Sub-Compact Wagons

1938-1980

Bantam, Crosley, Rambler, Pinto, Vega, Bobcat, Astre, Pacer

By Don Narus

Copyright 2014 Donald Narus
ISBN 978-1-62847-113-7

Published by
New Albany Books
2523 Pine Ridge Way S. B-1, Palm Harbor, Florida 34684

First Edition

Narus, Donald J. (Don)
1.Bantam, 2.Bobcat, 3.Crosley, 4.Pacer, 5.Pinto,6.Rambler, 7.Vega, 8.Woodies, 9. Station Wagons,

Contents

Published and printed in the United States of America

www.newalbanybooks.com

Photos and Credits

The images reproduced in this book are digital, direct download digital jpg images of various sizes which are formatted to fit. Some are originally black and white (usually Factory or Archived Photos). Others are color converted to black and white using a greyscale process. While all images were necessary to the content of this book their quality varies. The best images available at the time, for the example shown, were chosen. Every attempt was made to provide the best image. We also realize that photos are subjective. If better images or a conversion process becomes available after initial publication, they will be used in later revised editions.

Thanks to the following whose contribution has made this book possible:
John Tuthill, Mark Becker, John Lee, Douglas Englin, Flickr/PintoPower, Steve Manning net-a-car, Auto-Lit.Com, sport suburban, Brule Laker, Greg, Gjerdinger, conceptcarz.com, Crosley Automobile Club, Shotgun Taylor, Go Motors, Flickr.com, Wikimedia.com, Pat Jones, Cauldron Graphics, Wikipedia.com, Curbside Classics, Station Wagon Finder.com, RedTiger.com Tom Klockau. GM Photo Shop, Ford Motor Company, Pontiac Motor Division, Lincoln-Mercury Division, Detroit Public Library Auto Archives. AMC Motors. Every effort was made to identify all contributors, if we have missed anyone, please accept our sincere apologies and many thanks for your contribution. conceptcarz.com, Flickrriver.com

Front Cover: 1950 Rambler, American Motors photo
Rear Cover: 1947 Crosley Motors magazine ad

Introduction

Before the term "Compact" and "Sub-Compact" car were coined there was simply the small car. In this book we are going to cover the dreamers, the innovators and the players in the auto segment known as the "Sub-Compact". Specifically the Sub-Compact Station Wagons. (For the purposes of this book a Sub-Compact will be defined as a car with a wheelbase of 100 inch or less.)

In 1929 Sir Herbert Austin of England came to America with the plan to build cars based on English standards. In May of 1930 he started the American Austin Company in Butler, Pa. However America was not ready for a small car, the company closed in 1934. Austin super salesman Roy S. Evans took over the company expanded the line and renamed it American Bantam. His dream of an American small car lasted till 1941. The great depression and WW II certainly didn't help. America just wasn't ready to embrace the small car. However, Evans did come up with a vehicle that would become an Icon. The "Jeep"; proposed by the American Bantam Company to the U.S. Army in WW II, lives on to this day.

Powell Crosley Jr. built a small car when he was a teenager and had a dream of manufacturing cars. In 1939 Crosley founded The Crosley Motor Company. He met with limited success before WW II started. Then after the war with pent up demand in a sellers market the Crosley small car flourished only to fall prey to a fickle market. Once demand was met sales dropped and Crosley closed in 1952.

George Mason head of Nash Motors was fascinated with small cars, he reasoned that predecessors in this market had got it wrong. They were selling on price alone. Mason had a better idea. In 1950 Nash Motors launched the "Rambler". A 2-door, based on a 100 inch wheelbase with a lot of standard features. Initially a convertible was offered and was followed by a station wagon. Mason's idea of providing a reasonably comfortable car with seating for four and including a lot of standard features, instead of a lot of options, met with immediate success. Rambler had established a Sub-Compact market. During its five model year run Rambler sold over 135,000 station wagons. George Romney took over when Mason died and created the Compact car market with the 4-door 108 inch wheelbase Rambler. This drew the attention of the two big players. Ford and Chevrolet.

Ford and Chevrolet sat on the side lines and watched as Rambler sales continued to climb, then both Chevrolet and Ford launched their own Sub-Compacts.

The Chevrolet Vega was launched in 1971. Three models were available a 2-door sedan, a hatchback coupe and a station wagon called the "Kamback". The timing was right as 269,905 Vegas were sold that first year,. over 42,000 were Kamback station wagons.

The 97.0 inch wheelbase Vega, although plagued with quality problems from the start (mechanical and rust issues) flourished through 1977 and sold well over 2,000,000 units, of which 356,912 were station wagons. GM's Pontiac division launched its version of the Vega, called the Astre in 1975. Astre ended in 1977, it sold 38,788 station wagons.

Ford also launched it's Pinto Sub-Compact in 1971, initially with two models, both 2-door hatchbacks. A wagon was added in 1972. The Pinto was plagued with bad press, when some safety issues came into play, regarding its gas tank design. Ford chose to go to court instead of settling claims. Ford managed to overcome the bad press much as Chevrolet overcame its issues. Boosted by demand for small, economical small cars because of the oil embargo of the mid 1970's, Pinto's and Vega's continued to sell in great numbers.

By the end of its ten year run the Pinto sold over 900,000 station wagon units. In 1975 the Mercury Division of Ford launched its version of the Pinto called the Bobcat. The Bobcat was available in two models, a Runabout hatchback and a station wagon. Available from 1975-1980, 68,867 were sold

In 1977 AMC introduced the Pacer. An upscale Sub-Compact. The unique 2-door wagon rode on a 100 inch wheelbase. With a low belt line, the windows were very large, giving it unparalleled visibility. It was as wide as a Cadillac sedan and the passenger door was 4 inches wider than the drivers door. It was sometimes referred to as the "Fishbowl on Wheels". The wide stance provided big car comfort and increased cargo capacity. The Pacer was available from 1977-1980.

Don Narus

Bantam 1938-1941

The American Austin Company was founded by sir Herbert Austin of England. Roy S. Evans took over the failing company in 1935 and changed the name to American Bantam, The Bantam line was unveiled in 1936 with five models. A Roadster, Business Coupe 1 passenger, Business Coupe 2 passenger, Standard Coupe and a Deluxe Coupe. Prices ranged from $295. - $385. Total production for 1936 was just under 500 units.

For 1937 the range increased $385-$492. and total production had increased to 3,500 units. In 1938 a 2-door station wagon was introduced. It weighed in at 1,434 pounds and was priced at $565. Making it the highest priced model in the line-up. Only 53 were built*.

American Bantam had contracted Mifflinburg Body Company of Williamsburg, Pa to build the wagon bodies. All were constructed of Ash and Maple at a cost to Bantam of, $160. each. A little more than one quarter the selling price.

In 1939 ten models were available: A Roadster, DeLuxe Roadster, Business Coupe, 2-passenger Coupe, a Master 2-passenger Coupe, a Deluxe 2-passenger Coupe, a Foursome Roadster and the 2-door Station Wagon. The Wagon price remained unchanged at $565. It was powered by an In-Line 4 cylinder, 46.0 cu. in. 20hp engine. Coupled to a three speed manual transmission. Total sales slipped to 1,229 units, with the wagon as top seller with 219 units. Sales continued to drop and in 1940 only 800 total units were sold. Even with an increase of 22hp. the general public did not warm to the economy car. Only 138 total units were sold in 1941 of which 15 were wagons*. During this period Bantam built a utility prototype that they proposed selling to the Army.

In 1941 Bantam received a US Army contract to build the utility vehicle, which later became known as the "Jeep". But after the Pearl Harbor attack Willys and Ford, who had a greater capacity, took over the contract. Bantam did receive a contract to build two-wheel trailers for the Jeep, which kept the company afloat through WW II.

*According to American Austin/Bantam Club records, there were 53 chassis shipped in 1938, 219 in 1939 and 79 in 1940. I am assuming these were shipped to Mifflinburg for wagons. Records also show wagon production figures at 0 for 1938, 219 for 1939 and 95 for 1940. If my assumption is correct 53 wagons were built in 1938, 219 in '39, 79 in '40 and 15 in '41. There is no indication that the chassis shipped were used for anything else except station wagons.

1934 Austin Bantam Wagon

Is this a Prototype? Was it factory built? I have found no production record of a factory built wagon for 1934. But that is not to say that one was not built. Auto Company record keeping was pretty lax during the 30s and 40s. My guess is that it was built out of a coupe. Note the roof, spare mount and rear bumper, all consistent with a coupe, and no tail-gate only a lift-gate. A pretty neat car.

1938-39 American Bantam Wagon

This is a photo of a 1938 body titled as a 1939. the wagon was unchanged from 1938. Early 1939's used the 1938 hood which was accordion hinged. Later 1939 models and 1940 and 1941 models all used the single, down the center hinge. The wood bodies were all the same 1938-1941. Wagons were priced at $565.

The 1938 accordion hood is shown on the **(left)** early 1939 models used the same hood which was later changed to the single center hinge with fixed side panel shown on the **(right).** Buyers in the 30s and 40s were not as attuned to style as they were to dependability. So it was common practice in the industry to use up left over parts into the new calender year.

 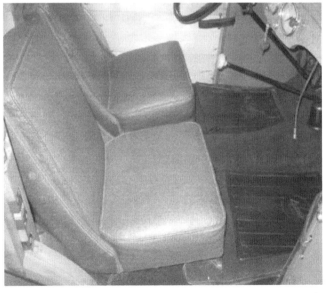

As you can see with the rear seat in place reduced the cargo area. A couple of pieces of luggage at best. The lift-gate/tail-gate combination provided easy access. All interiors were upholstered the same from 1938-1941.

1939 American Bantam Wagon

The 1939 American Bantam Station Wagon. The white wall tires, wheel rings, rear quarter window glass and hood ornament are all options. This is a late model with the "Butterfly" hood. There was no increase in the base price of $565. Note: the absence of running boards. Running boards were not standard or available as options.

The rear window is small because of the arch in the roof. The metal frame around the edge of the lift-gate is painted the body color. The large tailgate provides additional cargo carrying capacity. Front and rear bumpers are the same. Single tail light is standard.

 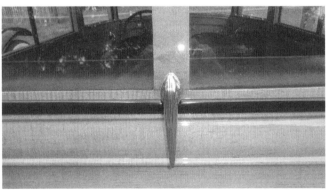

The spare is housed in a compartment below the tailgate. Door handles and lift-gate handle are the same. Simple brackets and off the shelf hardware were used throughout. To remove the rear seat a pair of wing nuts had to be removed from backrest bracket.

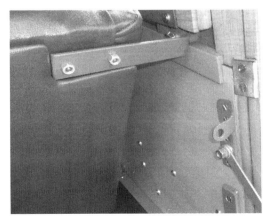  

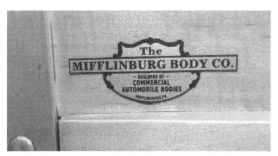

The interior was spartan. Plain leather seats and rubber floor mats. The mifflinburg tag was found at the bottom of the drivers door. The hood ornament resembles a '41 Chevy without the plastic. As with all wagons of the era, there is no headliner. The wood grain dash is actually a decal over steel. Dashboard is simple. There is no temperature gauge

1940 American Bantam Wagon

The 1940 model was unchanged including the $565. base price. The Engine size was increased to 50.1 cu in and rated at 22 hp. Mifflinburg continued to supply the wood body

Black wall tires and no options is exactly the way the Bantam came from the factory in 1940. A spartan, utility vehicle. The front fender mud guards were added later.

The Bantam was devoid of hood trim except for the small name plate on the side. Fit and finish was very good. The steering wheel was the same used in the WW II Bantam Jeep. Starter button, head light switch and manual choke; simple; functional. Off the shelf hardware continued to be used throughout. Gauges included: Fuel, Oil, and Ampere.

1941 American Bantam Wagon

Bantam's lined up at the Mifflinburg plant.   Only 15 were sold in 1941.

The proposed Bantam jeep was accepted by the U.S. Army; however, the production contract was given to Willys and Ford. Bantam did produce 3,000 Jeeps all of which were shipped to Russia. Bantam did receive a contract to produce Jeep Trailers. That contract kept the company afloat during the war years.

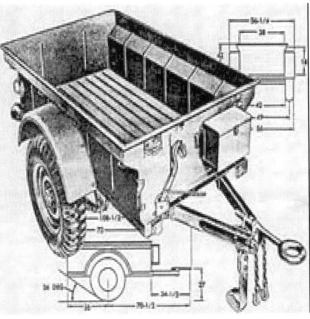

Bantam Related Miscellaneous

(Above) A prototype Panel Delivery with quarter windows. **(Below)** A 1936 Austin 10 open Cabriolet, 93 inch wheelbase, 30hp 1125cc engine. This custom one-of-kind "Woodie" roadster resembles a 1932 Ford. It is 18 inches longer than a Bantam. Builder and owner are unknown.

1938 American Bantam Wagon

Wheelbase: 75 Inches   Engine: 46.0 cu in, 4 cylinder, 20 hp, 3-speed

Model	Price	Built
60 Station Wagon 2-door	$565.	53*

1939 American Bantam Wagon

Wheelbase: 75 Inches   Engine: 46.0 cu in, 4 cylinder, 20 hp, 3-speed

Model	Price	Built
62 Station Wagon 2-door	$565.	219*

1940 American Bantam Wagon

Wheelbase: 75 Inches   Engine: 50.1 cu in, 4 cylinder, 22 hp, 3-speed

Model	Price	Built
65 Station Wagon 2-door	$565.	79*

1941 American Bantam Wagon

Wheelbase: 75 Inches   Engine: 50.1 cu in, 4 cylinder, 22 hp, 3-speed

Model	Price	Built
65 Station Wagon 2-door	$565.	15*

*Production information from American/Austin Bantam Club News Vol.3 #2 March-April 1993 Which included a chart of production numbers by year and model. The chart shows Chassis shipped as well as Station Wagons. The author has taken the chassis shipped and compared that to Station Wagons. In 1938 53 chassis were shipped, in 1939 it shows 219, in 1940 it shows 79. In 1939 the chassis shipped is exactly the same as Station Wagons built. Based on that correlation I have deduced that the chassis shipped were probably built into station wagons. I also took the photo that shows a lot full of wagons which more than likely was taken at the Mifflinburg Body Co I believe these are 1940 models, calculating the number of cars in the photo I came up with 75 which closely matches the 79 chassis production figure. Therefore,the wagon production figure for 1940 at 95 may have included 15 cars that were actually 1941 models. Encyclopedia of American Cars indicates that 138 cars, all models, were produced in 1941. 15 of those could have been wagons. Of course all of this is speculation.

Pricing and specification information from Encyclopedia of American Cars by Editors of Consumer Guide.

1938 - 1940 American Bantam Production

BODY STYLES YEARS:	1938	1939	1940	TOTAL
ROADSTER	512	404	55	971
MASTER COUPE	481	186	217	884
STANDARD COUPE	135	606	11	752
PANEL DELIVERY	415	479	216	1,110
PICK UP	230	235	115	580
CHASSIS	53	219	79	351
STATION WAGON		219	98	317
4 PASSENGER SPEEDSTER		308	15	323
BOULEVARD DELIVERY		70		70
HOLLYWOOD CONV. COUPE			134	134
STANDARD CONV. COUPE			60	60
RIVIERA 4 PASS. CONV			130	130
STANDARD 4 PASS. CONV.			60	60
BODY STYLE NOT IDENTIFIED	15	100 (EXPORT)		115
MISC BODIES	1	4		5
CAB OVER ENGINE		1		1
TOTALS:	1,842	2,831	1,190	5,863
VEHICLES SHIFTED TO NEXT MODEL YEAR	3	55		
SERIAL NUMBERS NOT USED OR VEHICLES NOT INSPECTED	157	455	38	650
	2,002	3,341	1,228	
MINUS VEHICLES TRANSFERRED FROM PREVIOUS YEAR		- 3	- 55	
SERIAL NUMBER RANGE	2,002	3,338	1,173	6,513

This is the chart that appeared in the March-April 1993 Vol.3 #2 issue of American Austin Bantam Club News, part of an article written by Charles Blackman furnished to the author by Bantam owner Mark Becker.

The article was an extensive search into the production of Bantam models produced from 1938 through 1941. The chart was assembled from information provided by Chet Hempfling a final inspector on the American Bantam production line, during those years hr kept records of every car that left the factory. Although wagon production figures are singled out in the chart, my contention is that the chassis figure is closer to actual wagon production. With that in mind, the difference between the chassis figure and the wagon figure for 1940 would indicate that 15 wagons were sold in 1941.

Crosley
1940-1942

Powel Crosley Jr. had a love affair with cars that traced back to his teenage years. After becoming a radio and refrigerator mogul he acted on his teenage crush and entered the auto manufacturing business in 1939. He introduced a Volkswagen like car on a 80 inch wheelbase. It was powered by a 2 cylinder engine and was priced at $325 - $350. and weighed less than half ton. The car was sold through hardware and appliance stores. By 1942 Crosley had built 5,000 cars.

Only two models were offered in 1939, a 2-passenger convertible coupe and a 4-passenger convertible sedan. The line-up expanded for 1940 to include a "Woodie" station wagon. Prices dropped to a low $299. Over-all styling was little changed. Headlights attached to the side of the hood, a small grille and free standing fenders. The interiors were spartan; a central speedometer with fuel and temp gauges. By the end of 1940 Crosley ran into a number of mechanical problems. To address the problems Paul Klotsch, a former Briggs Manufacturing Engineer was hired in 1941.

Klotsch improved the engine by redesigning the motor mounts, adding U-joints and revised the lubrication system. The improved engine was now rated at 12 hp. Sales improved to 2,289 units. In addition to the appliance stores cars were now sold through car dealers.

There were no changes for 1942. Prices increased to $468-$482. Only 1,029 units were built during the shortened war-time model year. During WW II Crosley developed a over-head 4 cylinder engine with a block made out of brazed copper and sheet steel for the U.S. Navy. It was called the "Cobra" and was successful in a number of applications. Crosley chose to use that engine in his postwar cars. Postwar production began in June of 1946. Problems quickly developed with the "Cobra" engine. Electrolysis had caused holes in the cylinder bores. Crosley immediately switched to a cast iron block, which solved the problem. For 1946 only two models were available; a four seat closed sedan and a convertible. The station wagon would return in 1947.

1940 Crosley Station Wagon

Introduced in 1940 the Crosley station wagon was priced at $450. which made it their most expensive model. Note: the interesting oval tailgate windows.

1941 Crosley Station Wagon

The 1941 Crosley station wagon was unchanged. <u>Note:</u> the tapered running board which did not protect the rear fender. and the interesting bumper brackets. The design was not unlike a European shooting break. the two piece tailgate provided ample access to the cargo area. The interior was spartan. It was priced at $496.

1942 Crosley "Liberty"

The new for 1942 "Liberty" 2-door sedan (coupe) that looked like a wagon. This would have been a "Black-out" car with painted trim. Mandated by material shortages and WW II government restrictions governing civilian auto production. At the end of January 1942, all auto production ended.

PICKUP DELIVERY $385⁰⁰

COVERED WAGON $399⁰⁰

PARKWAY DELIVERY $399

PANEL DELIVERY $435⁰⁰

STATION WAGON $450⁰⁰

CONVERTIBLE COUPE $299⁰⁰

CONVERTIBLE SEDAN $349⁰⁰

This 1942 ad shows all models available from 1940 through 1942 and introducing the all-new "Liberty" with an all-steel roof. It was a 2-door sedan (coupe) that looked like a station wagon. The Liberty carried 4 passengers on a wheelbase of 80 inches and powered by a 38.9 cu. in. In-Line 2 cylinder engine rated at 13.5hp. Exact number produced is unknown. With the United State entry into WW II, 1942 became a shortened model year for all auto makers. Production of civilian cars stopped at the end of January 1942 and total Crosley production, all models, was a meager 1,029 units.

1947 Crosley Station Wagon

There was no station wagon model available in 1946, the all-new slab sided design made its debut in 1947. It was a neat, clean design. Simulated wood panel were stamped into the sheet metal with wood grain decals. The windows were sliders all around. The tailgate window was enlarged one piece which did not fill the depressed steel stamping area. Bumpers were beefed up and splash pans added. Over-all it had a good, grown-up look. Priced at $929., 1,249 were sold.
It was the first American made all-steel station wagon. GM would follow in 1949.

1948 Crosley Station Wagon

Only the grille had changed for 1948. A nose cone and horizontal bars were added. It was still a sellers market and 1948 would be the best sales year for the station wagon. Priced at $929. (no increase) a total of 23,489 were sold.

Two large clock faces housed the gauges and the speedometer. A starter button on the far left. Radio controls were centered, speaker and glove box to the right.

Crosley
1949-1952

1949 became a buyers market. Supply was catching up with demand. The "Big Three" were unveiling there new post-war designs. All this hurt Crosley sales. The over all volume for Crosley dropped to 7,500 units. This was ironic in that the 1949 model was a much improved car. The station wagon looked a little like the 1949 Ford wagon, with a smooth hood and integral front fenders, with pronounced seal beam headlights.

Crosley's hasty, early attempt at disc brakes, which deteriorated quickly from exposure to road salt in 1949, coupled with its early problems with the "Cobra" engine added to it's decline in sales. Conventional drum brakes returned for 1951.

By 1950 Rambler had entered the Sub-Compact market. Customers were no longer interested in anything new Crosley had to offer. So a new vehicle like the "Farm-O-Road" did nothing to improve sales. The "Farm-O-Road" was an interesting vehicle, in appearance it looked like a miniature Jeep. A utility vehicle on a 63 inch wheelbase, priced at $795 it was available with all kinds of accessories that could allow it to tow a hay wagon or dig a ditch.

Two wagon models were available for 1950, the Standard 2-door wagon and the Super 2-door wagon, priced at $916. and $984. respectively. A total of 4,204 wagons were sold.

For 1951 a prop spinner was added to the grille. Which looked like a aftermarket attachment and did little to improve appearance. Prices were increased by $86 for the Standard wagon and $93 fro the super. Sales rose slightly to 4,500 units for both models.

By 1952 in was obvious that the American car buyer was no longer interested, in Crosley. With a meager production of 1,355 station wagons, and over-all production of 2.075 units, Crosley closed the door on auto production in July of 1952. General Tire and Rubber acquired the Crosley auto division and ultimately disposed of the operation.

1949 Crosley Station Wagon

A new grille, bumper guards and hood made up the facelift for 1949 which improved the over all appearance. It was priced at $894 and 3,803 were sold.

1950 Crosley Station Wagon

The 1950 Crosley Super station wagon. It was priced at $984 and featured a up graded interior of two tone vinyl and leatherette trim panels. It was a best seller.

Introduced in 1949 the new dashboard was carried over unchanged for 1950

1951 Crosley Station Wagon

A minor facelift was given the 1951 Crosley station wagon. A spinner was added to the upper grille bar and a new ornament graced the hood. Ample access to the cargo area. Roll up door glass and slider quarter windows. It was priced at $1,077 Nose spinner looked like an aftermarket add on. Bumper guards were optional. Twin tail/stop lights were embedded in the "C" posts.

The 1951 speedometer face was changed to red. **(Below)** dash with radio delete.

1952 Crosley Station Wagon

1952 was the last year for Crosley. The Super station wagon was unchanged. The addition of a roof rack increased cargo capacity. Wood grain decals, optional. <u>Note:</u> interesting application of a Crosley wagon as an in-door factory ambulance.

Indoor Ambulance

On duty 24 hours a day, a small ambulance can speed down the aisles of a big factory to pick up any worker who becomes sick or is injured. The ambulance, made from a Crosley station wagon, provides quick pickup service inside the Transformer Division plant of the Westinghouse Electric Corporation at Sharon, Pa. The factory is ¾ mile long.

One-of-a-Kind Miscellaneous Crosley

A 1949 Crosley convertible turned into a woodie by its owner. Note how the rear quarter wood trim frames out a fender with splash guard. Interesting!

1949 Crosley station wagon with real wood paneling applied to the sheet metal
<u>Note:</u> the bike carrier and luggage rack. This car was sold at auction for $27.000.

1940 Crosley Station Wagon
Wheelbase:80.0 Inches Engine: 38.9 cu in, In-Line 2 cylinder, 13.5hp

Model	Price	Built
2A Station Wagon 2-door	$450.	no wagon breakout

1941 Crosley Station Wagon

Model	Price	Built
CB41 Station Wagon 2-door	$496.	no wagon breakout

1942 Crosley Station Wagon

Model	Price	Built
CB42 Station Wagon 2-door	$582.	no wagon breakout

1947 Crosley Station Wagon
Wheelbase: 80.0 Inches Engine: 44.0 cu in, In-Line 4 cylinder, 26.5hp

Model	Price	Built
CC Station Wagon 2-door	$929.	1,249

1948 Crosley Station Wagon

Model	Price	Built
CC Station Wagon 2-door	$929.	23,480

1949 Crosley Station Wagon

Model	Price	Built
CD Station Wagon 2-door	$894.	3,803

1950 Crosley Station Wagon

Model	Price	Built
CD Standard Wagon 2-door	$916.	}4,204
CD Super Wagon 2-door	$984.	

1951 Crosley Station Wagon

Model	Price	Built
CD Standard Wagon 2-door	$1,002.	}4,500
CD Super Wagon 2-door	$1,077.	

1952 Crosley Station Wagon

Model	Price	Built
CD Standard Wagon 2-door	$1,002.	}1,355
CD Super Wagon 2-door	$1,077.	

Pricing and production information from Encyclopedia of American Cars by Consumers Guide

Rambler (Nash)
1950-1955

Nash President George Mason, had wanted a small car since Nash's merger with Kelvinator in 1937. After WW II Mason figured the time was right. As George Romney, Masons right hand man and later head of AMC, put it; "Their position (Ford and Chevrolet) was quite different from ours. It's one thing for a small company-a marginal firm- to pioneer a new concept and really push it. But its another thing for people who already have a big slice to begin pushing something that undercuts their basic market."

The new Nash Rambler was introduced on April 14, 1950. Initially only a convertible model was available. The wagon was added on June 23,1950. Due in part to a shorten model year sales got off to a slow start and only 11,428 Ramblers were sold that first year. However, with a full year under their belt Rambler sales reached 57,555 the following year.

Rambler used a L-head six, first developed for the 1941 Nash 600, as its power plant. The 172.6 cu in was rated at 82hp. A three speed manual transmission was standard. The new car was a first with unibody construction on a short wheelbase. The practical little 2-door station wagon, accounted for most of the Rambler sales through its five year run. Four adults could be seated comfortably with ample cargo capacity. The wagon like the convertible was loaded with options: Radio, custom steering wheel, turn signals, electric clock, courtesy lights, foam cushions with custom upholstery and wheel discs. It was priced at $1,808.

In 1951 two wagon models were available; the base wagon now called the Super Suburban priced at $1,885. and the Custom priced at 1,993. A total of 34,186 wagon were sold this year. The wagon was unchanged for 1952, the price of the Super Suburban rose to $2,003 and the Custom to $2,119. The higher priced Custom outsold the Super 9 to 1. From 1953 through 1955 the Rambler wagon received minor facelifts and gradual price increases. In 1954 a 4-door wagon was added with a longer wheelbase which put it in the "Compact" category.

In the early years of the all-steel wagons Rambler accounted for 22 percent of the wagon market. The 100 inch wheelbase Rambler was discontinued in 1956, only to be revived in 1958 as the Rambler American.

1950 Rambler Station Wagon

The 1950 Rambler Station Wagon was introduced on June 23, 1950. sitting on a 100 inch wheelbase it was larger then its then competitor Crosley. Although double the price of the Crosley the Rambler was a entirely new car, with more attractive styling with room for 5-passengers. It was priced at $1,808.

A stripped down version of the wagon, called the Deliveryman was available at a reduced price. It was popular with salesmen, and tradesmen, a utility hauler.

The Rambler dash was clean and functional. A speed-o cluster sat in front of the driver. The steering wheel was large, the same used in the Statesman. A unique speaker grille was positioned between the two large radio dials, a drawer served as the glove box. Two tone vinyl upholstery finished off the interior.

1951 Rambler Station Wagon

Sales jumped in 1951 with 28,618 Custom models sold. New for this year was the Super Suburban model priced below the custom as a entry level wagon. 5,568 Suburbans were sold and total Rambler wagons sales reached 34,186.

1952 Rambler Station Wagon

The 1952 Custom Wagon was unchanged. The skirted front fender became a Rambler trade mark. Priced at $2,119 over 19,800 were sold. Note: the optional flying lady hood ornament. The fender/cowl air dams were non-functional. **(Below)** New for 1952 was the special edition Greenbriar. Shown here with golfing great Sam Snead.

The 1952 Super Suburban wagon, 2,970 were sold at a base price of $2,003 FOB. The quarter windows situated at the rear seat were locking sliders. Optional wood grain decal was applied to the frame around the windows and tailgate.

1953 Rambler Station Wagon

The 1953 Custom Wagon received a new grille and hood. It was priced at $2,119. There was ample room for four passengers with luggage and room to spare.

She drives a Rambler

PHOTOGRAPHY BY COSTA NIKOLAUS

"The beautiful Pinin Farina styling and custom appointments of the Nash Rambler make it appropriate for meeting the most distinguished guest."

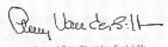

Perry Vanderbilt

Author of Best-selling "Amy Vanderbilt's Complete Book of Etiquette"

What woman doesn't thrill to know she can be smart and distinctive... yet still be practical!

Here, in the beautiful new Nash Rambler for 1953, is her perfect answer for personal transportation. Smoothly styled in the continental trend by Pinin Farina, world's foremost car designer, and smartly tailored by Madame Helene Rother, the Rambler has a personality all its own.

To its continental beauty, add the practicality of the easiest handling and parking you've ever known... Dual-Range Hydra-Matic Drive... touches like Reclining Seats and a sliding Glove Drawer... plus fuel economy that's so easy on a budget. Then you'll know why this custom compact car has set a new vogue in motor cars.

Your Nash dealer invites you to join the many social leaders like Miss Vanderbilt— now driving her third Rambler— and enjoy a Rambler of your very own.

The 1953 *Nash* Rambler
CONVERTIBLE · HARDTOP
STATION WAGON

Nash Motors, Division Nash-Kelvinator Corporation, Detroit 32, Mich.

1953 Super Suburban wagon with optional flying lady hood ornament,$2,003.
(Below) The Deliveryman UV continued to be available but only 9 were sold.

1954 Rambler Station Wagon

The 1954 Rambler Custom Wagon was unchanged 2,202 were sold at $1,950.

The 1954 Rambler Suburban wagon only 504 were sold at a price tag of $1,800. Window frames and tailgate were painted a contrasting color or covered with a wood grain decal.

1955 Rambler Station Wagon

1955 was the last year for the 100 inch wheelbase Rambler Subcompact giving way to the 108 inch 4-door wagons. Only one wagon model was offered for 1955; the Suburban. it was priced at $1,771 and only 2,379 were sold. In addition to the wagon the Deliveryman Utility was still available but a scant 14 were sold.

1950 Rambler Station Wagon

Wheelbase: 100.0 Inches Engine: 172.6 cu in In-Line 6 cylinder, 82hp

Model	Price	Built
5024 Custom Wagon 2-door	$1,808.	1,712
5004 Deliveryman Wagon	$1,100.	N/A

1951 Rambler Station Wagon

Wheelbase: 100.0 Inches Engine: 172.6 cu in, In-Line 6 cylinder, 82hp

5114 Super Suburban Wagon	$1,885.	5,588
5124 Custom Wagon 2-door	$1,993.	28,618
5104 Deliveryman Wagon	$1,173.	1,569

1952 Rambler Station Wagon

Wheelbase: 100.0 Inches Engine: 172.6 cu in, In-Line 6cylinder, 82hp

5214 Super Suburban Wagon	$2,003.	2,970
5224 Custom Wagon 2-door	$2,119.	15,464
5224 Greenbriar SE Wagon		4,524
2204 Deliveryman Wagon	$1,892.	1,248

1953 Rambler Station Wagon

Wheelbase: 100.0 Inches Engine: 184.0 cu in, In-Line 6 cylinder, 85hp
  Optional Engine: 195.6 cu in, In-Line 6 cylinder, 90hp, Automatic Transmission

5314 Super Suburban Wagon	$2,003.	1,114
5324 Custom Wagon 2-door	$2,515.	7,035
5324 Greenbriar SE Wagon		3,536
2304 Deliveryman Wagon	$1,892.*	9

1954 Rambler Station Wagon

Wheelbase: 100.0 Inches Engine: 184.0 cu in, In-Line 6 cylinder, 85hp
  Optional Engine: 195.6 cu in, In-Line 6 cylinder, 90hp Automatic Transmission

5414 Super Suburban Wagon	$1,800.	504
5424 Custom Wagon 2-door	$1,950.	2,202
2404 Deliveryman Wagon	$1,692.*	56

1955 Rambler Station Wagon

Wheelbase: 100.0 Inches Engine: 195.6 cu in, In-Line 6 cylinder, 90hp

5514 DeLuxe Suburban Wagon	$1,771.	}2,379
5514-1 Super Suburban Wagon	$1,869	
2504 Deliveryman Wagon	$1,613.*	14

*Estimated pricing based on price adjustments for the Suburban wagon
Pricing and production information from Encyclopedia of American Cars by Consumer Guide and Standard Catalog of American Cars by John Gunnell

Pinto (Ford)
1971-1980

In answer to the growing Sub-Compact market, Ford introduced the Pinto in 1971, to compete with Chevrolet Vega and AMC Gremlin. Two models were available initially, a 2-door Sedan and a 2-door Runabout. The market responded favorably to the pinto and 352,402 were sold. That same year Chevy Vega sold 269,905 and the Germlin sold 53,480. Pinto outsold both Vega and Gremlin combined, by 29,00 units.

In 1972 a Pinto Station Wagon was added to the line-up. The 2-door wagon resembled a scaled down Ford Country Squire. Standard equipment included vent less door windows, high back bucket seats, all-vinyl interior, floor mounted shifter and rack and pinion steering. Two engine options were available, a standard British built 98 cu.in. 54hp overhead valve 4 cylinder and a German built 122 cu. in. 86hp 4 cylinder, which was the more popular choice. A Cruise-O-Matic automatic transmission was available with the larger engine. 101,483 wagons were sold affirming Fords status as the "wagonmaster".

There were no changes for 1973 except that front and rear bumper guards were made standard. The base price was increased by $78. and sales climbed to 217,763 units. For 1974 energy absorbing bumpers were added which changed the overall look. The simulated wood grain panels were made optional and became part of the Luxury Decor Group. In 1975 a 2.8 liter V-6 was available only with Cruise-O-Matic. The V-6 developed 97hp. Combined sales of 4 cylinder and V-8 models 90,763.

For 1976 the Pinto received a facelift. A one piece plastic egg crate grille and bright headlight bezels. A chrome strip was added to the leading edge of the hood and FORD block letters were added above the grille. Tinted glass was standard. A tailgate warning light was added and quarter windows had a flip-out feature. In 1977 the Pinto received another facelift with a restyled sloping hood. A new model, the Cruising Wagon was added. It was aimed at the growing youth market and included a front spoiler, styled wheels, sports graphics and a carpeted cargo compartment. The Package sold for an additional $416. New paint and interior colors made up most of the changes for 1978. The Cruising package continued for 1979 and was revised in 1980. For 1979 Standard equipment included a AM radio, power brakes, Electric rear defroster and tinted glass.

1980 was the last year for the Pinto, it would be replaced with the Escort in 1981 with no wagon model. The Wagon model would return in 1982 and would continue through 1999.

Pinto Wagon
is the basic wagon idea all over again:
lots of space for little money.

When Ford pioneered the station wagon in 1929, we simply combined a durable, economical car with a lot of space in back.

That's exactly what we've done with the Pinto Wagon.

We've taken the durable, economical Pinto—and given it over 60 cubic feet of cargo space. (Vega Kammback and VW Squareback give you about 50.) The rear seat folds down, the lift gate swings up out of the way, the spare tire is stored under the floor to maximize cargo space.

Under the hood, you'll find a 2000cc overhead cam engine as standard equipment. Also a fully synchronized 4-speed transmission. (You can opt for automatic, of course.) Plus extra strength universal and ball joints, starter motor, rear wheel bearings.

Front disc brakes are standard on Pinto Wagon. Along with rack-and-pinion steering, a body that's welded into one solid piece of steel, and a rear suspension specially designed for load-carrying.

In short, the Pinto Wagon is ideal for people who want a basic economy car that carries more —or a wagon that costs less.

Shown here is the Pinto Wagon with Squire Option, optional whitewall tires, luggage rack, deluxe bumper group, automatic transmission.

Pinto Wagons for '73, at your Ford Dealer's. Better idea for safety...buckle up!

When you get back to basics, you get back to Ford.

FORD PINTO

FORD DIVISION *Ford*

1972 Pinto Station Wagon

The 1972 Pinto Station Wagon featured simulated wood paneling, and a roof rack. Generous cargo capacity for whatever the job. Priced at $2,265.over 101,000 sold

The 1972 Pinto Station Wagon was introduced on February 24, 1972. Shown here at the Chicago Auto Show. The Pinto was one of three wagons offered in 1972.

1973 Pinto Squire Wagon

1973 Pinto Squire Wagon was unchanged. Young family's loved it Priced at $2,343. a total of 217,783 sold, a record second year it was a home rune.

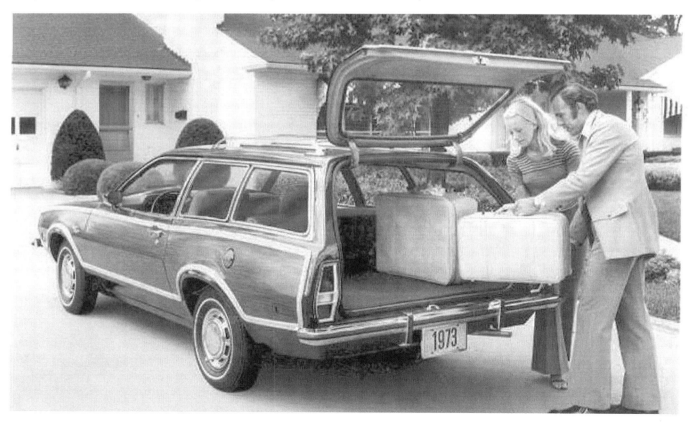

The 1973 Pinto Wagon came with a lot of standard features which were found in higher priced wagons. Cruise-O-Matic transmission was an available option.

The cargo area had wall to wall carpeting, and over 57 cubic feet of capacity.

1973 Pinto 4-Door Prototype Wagon

Apparently in 1973 Ford considered building a 4-door version of the Pinto wagon. The over-all dimensions seem to be unchanged. They narrowed the front door and added a rear door. It seems that only the one prototype was built.

It looks like the rear door has a fixed window. There is no window crank. A modified front door panel. On close examination it appears that there is only one rear door. Drivers side. Apparently only to be photographed on the divers side.

1974 Pinto Squire Wagon

The 1974 Pinto Squire, it was the third year without change and sales were better than ever. Another record with 237,394 units. The base price increased by $428.

The Pinto Squire had an up-scale all-vinyl interior with wood grain trim and several color choices. Shown here with Cruise-O-Matic transmission. It could accommodate four adults comfortably with ample cargo capacity.

1974 Pinto Standard Wagon

The Pinto Wagon could be had without the Squire package which was optional at $241. Although part of the package, the roof rack could be ordered separately.

The standard Pinto interior without the Luxury Decor Group, which included the wood grain trim. The AM radio was a $61 option. The heater was standard.

A fully carpeted cargo area. Rear Panel speakers were options. The optional rear roof spoiler could be had with or without the roof rack. Lots of room. Easy access.

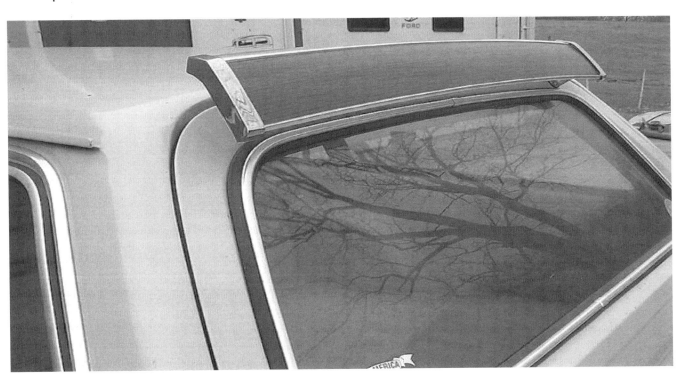

1975 Pinto Squire Wagon

Once again no changes. Price increased by $382. Sales dropped below 100,000.

D.   E.   F.

Interior options continued unchanged. **(Below)** the standard dash, no wood grain trim. Manual 3-speed transmission with floor mounted shifter. Optional AM radio.

Ample seating for four. Cloth and vinyl seating trim option with a choice of colors.

With the rear seat back folded cargo space was big enough for 4 x 8 plywood sheeting. The full size spare tire was housed in a well below the cargo floor.

1976 Pinto Squire Wagon

The 1976 Pinto Squire wagon with 4 cylinder 92hp engine was priced at $3,671. Pinto increased its miles per gallon for 1976 prompting the marketing of the 4 cylinder version as the MPG wagon. New vinyl-cloth interiors were available in bright plaids or bright stripes. The stripe version is shown here.

1976 Pinto Standard Wagon

The face-lifted 1976 featured a new grille and hood. Roof Rack and spoiler,options

1977 Pinto Cruising Wagon

The Pinto Cruising Wagon was introduced this year aimed at the youth market. Standard features included a front spoiler, styled wheels and sport equipment. Special paint and graphics were optional. It was priced at $3,964.

1977 Pinto Squire Wagon

The face lifted 1977 Pinto Squire Wagon featured quad parking lights. It was priced at $3,891. Wire wheel covers are optional. Sales continued to slip.

1977 Pinto Standard Wagon

1977 Pinto Standard Wagon, priced at $3,548. Note absence of bumper guards and rubber rub trim on the bumpers. Roof rack and rally wheels are options.

1978 Pinto Squire Wagon

1. Critical areas around lights and grille are dent, chip and scratch resistant...and absolutely rustproof!

2. Scheduled maintenance reduced 75% over the past five years.*

3. 33 MPG highway, 23 MPG city (EPA ratings).

4. DuraSpark Ignition. No points or condenser to replace.

5. Unit-body construction.

6. Woodgrain vinyl paneling.

7. Roomy cargo area (cargo volume index 57.2 cubic feet).

8. Flipper rear side windows.

9. Low sticker price.

10. Electro-dip corrosion protection.

11. Sporty suspension system.

12. 4-speed floor-mounted transmission (standard). SelectShift automatic (optional).

13. Precise rack and pinion steering.

14. Power front disc brakes.

15. Larger standard engine (2.3 litre, 4-cylinder cast iron) than Datsun F-10 Sportswagon, Toyota Corolla and Corona.

16. Even larger optional engine (2.8 litre V-6) for even more performance.

Pinto Squire Wagon

The 1978 Pinto Squire Wagon was unchanged, price increased by $452. to $4.343.

1978 Pinto Standard Wagon

The 1978 Pinto Standard Wagon without the optional roof rack sold for $4,028.

1978 Pinto Cruising Wagon

A new Cruising package was available which included a colored paint stripping, front spoiler, styled wheels, dual sport mirrors and steel side panels. The Cruising Wagon option cost $365. Graphics cost an extra $59. Roof rack another $59.

1979 Pinto Squire Wagon

Pinto received a new grille, hood and head light bezels which incorporated a square head lamp and large parking lights. It was priced $4,654. Over an eight year period the base price of the Pinto wagon had risen by $2,389.

1979 Pinto Cruising Wagon

The Cruising Wagon received a new set of Graphics for 1979, the wagon sold for $4,668. The interior was smart and youthful with two tone colors, pattern seats.

1979 Pinto Standard Wagon

A new, bare bones wagon was introduced in 1979. The "Pony", it was no frills and priced at $3,899 with 4 cylinder engine, 3-speed manual transmission and black-out grille it was $439 less than the Standard Pinto wagon.

1980 Pinto Squire Wagon

1980 was the last year for the Pinto Wagon over a nine model year period 977,504 were sold. No changes for 1980 and only three models available.

1980 Pinto Cruising Wagon

The Pinto Cruising Wagon package continued to be available, priced at $5,359.

1980 Pinto Standard Wagon

The Standard wagon and Pony version were available priced at $5,004 and $4,627. respectively. The roof rack, fog lights and pop-up sunroof were optional.

1972 Pinto Station Wagon

Wheelbase: 94.2 Inches Engine: 122.0 cu in, In-Line 4 cylinder, 86hp.

Model	Price	Built
12 Squire Wagon 2-door	$2,265.	101,483

1973 Pinto Station Wagon

Wheelbase: 94.2 Inches Engine: 122.0 cu in In-Line 4 cylinder, 83hp.

Model	Price	Built
12 Squire Wagon 2-door	$2,343.	217,763

1974 Pinto Station Wagon

Wheelbase: 94.2 Inches Engine: 122.0 cu in In-Line 4 cylinder, 80hp

Model	Price	Built
12 Squire Wagon 2-door	$2,771.	237,394

1975 Pinto Station Wagon

Wheelbase: 94.7 Inches Engine: 140.0 cu in In-Line 4 cylinder, 83hp

Model	Price	Built
12 Squire Wagon 2-door	$3,153.	90,763

1976 Pinto Station Wagon

Wheelbase: 94.7 Inches Engine: 140.0 cu in In-Line 4 cylinder, 88hp

Engine: 170.0 cu in V-6, 90hp, Cruise-O-Matic Trans

Model	Price	Built
12 Standard 2-door	$4,028.	}52,269
12 Squire Wagon 2-door	$4,343.	

Pricing and production information from Encyclopedia of American Cars by Consumers Guide and Standard Catalog of Ford by John Gunnell

1977 Pinto Station Wagon

Wheelbase: 94.7 Inches   Engine: 140.0 cu in In-line 4 cylinder, 89hp
Optional Engine: 170.8 cu in V-6, 93hp. Cruise-O-Matic Transmission

Model	Price	Built
12 Standard Wagon 2-door	$3,548.	}79,499
12 Squire Wagon 2-door	$3,891	
12 Cruising Wagon 2-door	$3,964.	

1978 Pinto Station Wagon

Wheelbase: 94.7 Inches Engine: 140.0 cu in, In-Line 4 cylinder, 88hp
Optional Engine: 170.0 cu in V-6, 90hp, Cruise-O-Matic Transmission

Model	Price	Built
12 Standard Wagon 2-door	$4,028.	}52,269
12 Squire Wagon 2-door	$4,343.	
12 Cruising Wagon 2-door	$4,159.	

1979 Pinto Station Wagon

Wheelbase: 94.7 Inches Engine: 140.0 cu in In-Line 4 cylinder, 88hp
Optional Engine: 170.0 cu in V-6, 102hp, Cruise-O-Matic Transmission

Model	Price	Built
12 Pony Wagon 2-door	$3,899.	}53,846
12 Standard Wagon 2-door	$4,338.	
12 Squire Wagon 2-door	$4,654	
12 Cruising Wagon 2-door	$4,668.	

1980 Pinto Station Wagon

Wheelbase: 94.7 Inches Engine: 140.0 cu in In-Line 4 cylinder, 88hp

Model	Price	Built
12 Pony Wagon 2-door	$4,627.	}39,159
12 Standard Wagon 2-door	$5,004.	
12 Squire Wagon 2-door	$5,320.	
12 Cruising Wagon 2-door	$5,359.	

Pricing and production information from Encyclopedia of American Cars by Consumer Guide

Vega/Monza (Chevrolet)
1971-1980

Throughout the 1970's Chevrolet was number one, except for 1970-71 when it ran second to Ford. With the strength of its position Chevrolet could do no wrong and when it did make a blunder it was able to shake if off with little more than a shrug. And so it was with the introduction of the Sub-compact, Vega. Which was looked upon as Chevy's biggest blooper of the decade, managed to hang on for seven model years with respectable numbers.

At the time Vega looked like a perfect fit when introduced in 1971. It rode on a 97 inch wheelbase, which was the shortest in Chevy history. It had a Camaro like front end and was available in three models: a 2-door Hatchback sedan, A Hatchback coupe and a "Kammback" wagon. This was Chevys latest attempt to counter Ford's new Pinto.

In its first year Chevy sold 42,793 Vega Kammback wagons. Ford had no Pinto wagon in 1971. In 1972 a total of 71,957 Vega wagons were sold. In comparison Ford sold 101,483 Pinto wagons. In 1973 Vega wagon sales had improved to the tune of 102,751. A more than respectable showing.

In 1974 the Vega received a facelift, with new hood, grille and energy absorbing bumpers. Vega's over-all appearance was changed with the addition of the Estate wagon. A trim level with Di-Noc (decal) wood grain side panels. Creating a faux woodie. The Estate wagon perked additional interest and helped increase over-all wagon sales to 115,337units.

By 1976 sales had taken a nose dive. With only 54,049 wagon units sold and 160,524 over-all, compared to Pinto sales of 207,092 the hand writing was on the wall. 1977 would be the last year for the Vega, giving way to a new model called the Monza. Introduced in 1978 on the same wheelbase of 97 inches, included a wagon which did not fair well. In its first year only 2,478 were sold. The sub-compact wagon experiment would end in 1980.In its final year 15,190 Monza wagons were sold. It wasn't enough to continue.

1971 Vega Station Wagon

A Camaro like front end created the base styling of the Vega. The wagon was called the Kamback. Over 42,700 were sold at a base price of $2,328. Some of its features included: high back bucket front seats, custom cloth interior and of all things an optional glove box, and an optional Turbo-Hydramatic transmission.

The 1971 Vega was officially "Chevrolet Vega 2300". The Kamback Wagon was model 14115, it was priced at $2,230. and a total of 42,793 were sold

1971 Vega Panel Express Wagon

The Vega Panel Express, a wagon variant, was considered a truck. It was aimed at the small business market. Standard features included a flat steel cargo floor with storage compartment, (there were no rear seats) and a single drivers seat (the passenger seat was optional). In its first year 7,800 were sold.

1972 Vega Station Wagon

The "Chevrolet Vega 2300" designation was replaced with a simple, "Vega by Chevrolet". Model number was now 1V15. There were no changes for 1972. 72,000 units were sold at a price tag fo $2,333. A slight increase over 1971.

1972 Vega Panel Express Wagon

If you want to save money on things like initial cost, gasoline, insurance and maintenance, look what Vega can do for you.

It takes you about 25 miles on a gallon of gas.

With the standard engine and transmission, that's what we got in our highway driving tests.

So why pay for a big truck when Vega can save you money carrying things like pizzas, photostats or flowers. There are dozens of uses for a light-weight, compact delivery truck.

Particularly if you have to get into tight places like delivery entrances, indoor garages and city traffic. If you need a truck, but not two tons of truck, you need Vega.

Parks with 8 feet left over.

Overall length of the Panel Express is only a couple of inches over 14 feet. That means it uses up less than two-thirds of a standard parking place. And it has a turning diameter of only 33 feet just in case you have to make a U-turn to get to that parking space.

<u>Note:</u> The Panel Express had low back front seats, and no rear seats.

A simple modification; removing the rear seat, replacing the quarter windows with steel panels, created the Panel Express. Shown here with a 3-speed manual.

1973 Vega Station Wagon

For the third year no changes were made. A GT model was available with special badge, stylized wheel and special interior. Over-all it was the basic wagon trimmed out. 1973 was the best sales year for Vega over 102,000 were sold.

The Vega Estate Wagon, with wood grain decal side trim and up-graded interior, was introduced mid-year to compete with the Ford's Pinto Squire wagon.

1973 Vega Panel Express Wagon

The Panel Express not only made good economic sense for commercial use but it was an inexpensive Beach Buggy. Room for two surf boards, snorkeling gear, two adults, a cooler, picnic basket, blankets and firewood. Perfect!,

Panel Express

1974 Vega Station Wagon

1974 ushered in a major face lift. A revised front end and government mandated 5 mph bumpers which added 6 inches to the over-all length. New slanted hood with a pressed, louvered steel panel, replacing the egg crate grille. The V15 Estate Wagon was priced at $2,976 and 27,089 were sold.

1974 Vega Panel Express Wagon

The versatile 1974 Vega Panel Express wagon. Sales up slightly, 4,287 were sold.

1975 Vega Station Wagon

There were no major changes for this year. A heavy rubber rub strip was added to the front and rear bumpers. New options included: power brakes and tilt wheel. 8,659 Estate wagons were sold at a price tag of $$3,244. FOB Lordstown, Ohio.

The Vega GT station wagon was market ploy aimed at young buyers. A popular choice, with color keyed rally wheels, chrome trim rings, smart GT badges.

A four speed manual transmission, a four spoke all black rally wheel, pleated vinyl seats and door panels all added to the appeal of the GT. Fully carpeted cargo bay.

'75 CHEVY VEGA PANEL EXPRESS

1975 would be the final year for the Vega Panel Express. There were no major changes and no up-grades. Only 1,525 were sold.

1976 Vega Station Wagon

The 1976 Vega received a facelift which included a Chevy 'Bow Tie' emblem,wider grille, and revised headlamp bezels, all made out of corrosion resistant material.

1976 Vega Nomad Station Wagon

New for 1976 was the Limited Edition Vega Nomad Wagon. It featured re-styled side windows and optional tinted "Sky-Roof" (pop-up sunroof). <u>Note:</u> the Nomad script badges on the wider "B" pillar and tailgate. Rear quarter window was fixed.

1977 Vega Station Wagon

1977 would be the final year for the Vega. During its seven year run the Vega was plagued with rust problems, ironically in its final year it received extensive anti-rust improvements which included galvanized fenders and rocker panels.

The Roof Spoiler was an option which could be had with or without the roof rack. The Estate Wagon option included wood grain trim on the exterior panels.

A velor cloth interior was optional as well as the Hydra-matic transmission. 28,642 Vega Station Wagons were sold in 1977 at a price of $3,522 for the standard model and $3,745. for the Estate Wagon.

1978 Monza Station Wagon

The 1978 Monza successor to the Vega, was in fact a Vega with a new grille. The Monza Estate wagon was one of two wagon models available. Only 2,478 sold.

The 1978 Monza Standard wagon was priced at $3,868 and sold a total of 24,255

1979 Monza Station Wagon

1979 was the final year for Chevrolet's Sub-Compact wagon. Only one model was offered, the Monza Standard wagon. priced at $4,167, total sold 15,190. Thus ended the Sub-Compact wars of the 1970s.

1971 Vega Station Wagon

Wheelbase:97.0 Inches Engine: 140.0 cu in, In-Line 4 cylinder, 90hp

Optional Engine: 140.0 cu in, In-Line4 cylinder, 110hp

Model	Price	Built
1V15 Station Wagon 2-door	$2,285.	71,957
Panel Express 2-door		7,800

1972 Vega Station Wagon

Wheelbase: 97.0 Inches Engine: 140.0 cu in, In-Line 4 cylinder, 80hp

Optional Engine:: 140.0 cu in, In-Line 4 cylinder, 90HP

V15 Station Wagon 2-door	$2,285.	71,957
Panel Express 2-door		4,114

1973 Vega Station Wagon

Wheelbase: 97.0 Inches Engine: 140.0 cu in, In-Line 4 cylinder, 72hp

Optional Engine: 140.0 cu in, In-Line4 cylinder, 85hp

V-15 Station Wagon 2-door	$2,323.	102,751
Panel Express 2-door		n/a

1974 Vega Station Wagon

Wheelbase: 97.0 Inches Engine: 140.0 cu in, In-Line 4 cylinder, 74hp

Optional Engine: 140.0 cu in, In-LIne 4 cylinder, 85hp

V15 Station Wagon 2-door	$2,748.	88,248
V15 Estate Wagon 2-door	$2,976.	27,089
Panel Express 2-door		4,287

1975 Vega Station Wagon

Wheelbase: 97.0 Inches Engine: 140.0 cu in, In-Line 4 cylinder, 78hp

Optional Engine: 140.0 cu in, In-Line 4 cylinder 87hp

V15 Station Wagon 2-door	$3,016.	47,474
V15 Estate Wagon 2-door	$3,244.	8,659
Panel Express 2-door		1,448

Pricing and production information from Encyclopedia of American Cars by Consumer Editors and Wikipedia

1976 Vega Station Wagon

Wheelbase: 97.0 Inches Engine: 140.0 cu in, In-Line 4 cylinder, 70hp

Optional Engine: 140.0 cu in, In-Line 4 cylinder, 84hp

Model	Price	Built
V15 Station Wagon 2-door	$3,227.	46,114
V15 Estae Wagon 2-door	$3,450.	7,935

1977 Vega Station Wagon

Wheelbase: 97.0 Inches Engine: 140.0 cu in, In-Line 4 cylinder, 84hp

Model	Price	Built
V15 Station Wagon 2-door	$3,227.	25,181
V15 Estate Wagon 2-door	$3,745.	3,461

1978 Monza Station Wagon

Wheelbase: 97.0 Inches Engine: 151.0 cu in, In-Line 4 cylinder, 85hp

Optional Engine: 196.0 cu in, V-6 cylinder, 90hp

Model	Price	Built
M15 Station Wagon 2-door	$3,868.	24,255
M15 Estate Wagon 2-door	$4,102.	2,478

1979 Monza Station Wagon

Wheelbase: 97.0 Inches Engine: 151.0 cu in, In-LIne 4 cylinder, 90hp

Optional Engine: 196.0 cu in, V-6 cylinder, 105hp

Model	Price	Built
M-15 Station Wagon 2-door	$3,868.	15,190

Pricing and production information from Encyclopedia of American Cars by Editors Consumer Guide and Wikipedia

Bobcat (Mercury)
1975-1980

In 1975 the Lincoln-Mercury Division of Ford Motor Company introduced the "Bobcat". The Mercury version of the Ford Pinto. The Sub-Compact was a needed addition to full fill the mpg requirements mandated by the government. The Bobcat was available as a hatchback runabout and a station wagon. This was Mercury's first entry into the Sub-Compact field. It was a half hearted attempt. Only one trim level was available; the "Villager", a squire like trim package. The bright trim surrounding the wood grain side panel decals immediately set off the Bobcat from its Pinto cousin. The Bobcat Villager was priced at $3,481. and a total of 13,583 units were sold in its introductory year. The standard power plant was a 140.0 cu.in. In-Line 4 cylinder rated at 83hp. With a 170.8 cu.in. 97hp V-6 as an available option.

The Bobcat wagon for 1976 was unchanged in appearance. Horsepower increased to 92 in the standard 4 cylinder engine. The same engine used in the Pinto. A 100hp V-6 was an available option. The price was increased by $162. and 18,731 units were sold. There would be no significant change in the Bobcat until 1979.

Two trim levels, the standard and the villager continued for 1978 with a significant increase in pricing. The standard wagon increased by $483. and the villager by $752. Sales dropped to 8,840 units.

The Bobcat received a substantial face lift in 1979. The Headlights and parking lights were integrated into the grille which stretched across the entire front. A new slopping hood and front fenders. Prices once again were increased.

1980 marked the end of the Bobcat. It was unchanged in its final year. The standard wagon sold for $5,070 and the villager for $5,183. Only 5,547 sold. The Bobcat was replaced by the Lynx in 1981 with no wagon. A Sub-Compact wagon returned in 1982 with four trim levels, sales jumped to 23,835 units. The Lynx was dropped in 1987, ending Sub-Compact wagons.

1975 Bobcat Station Wagon

A variant of the Pinto, the Bobcat Villager wagon was introduced in 1975. It was the only wagon model available. It sold for 3,481 and a total of 13,583 were sold.

The Bobcat Villager wagon was available with an all-vinyl upholstered interior and a wood grain trimmed dashboard. The automatic transmission was optional.

1976 Bobcat Station Wagon

In 1976 a wide heavy duty front bumper rub strip was added. Stylized wheels were optional. The Bobcat's utility proved to be versatile.

The Bobcat Villager wagon had a upgraded all-vinyl interior. Front bucket seats with adjustable head rests. The radio was optional the heater was standard.

1977 Bobcat Station Wagon

The 1977 Bobcat featured an aluminum bumper with bumper guards and narrow rubber rub strip. The roof rack with rear spoiler was optional. The rear quarter windows were split , the front half swung out for ventilation.

1978 Bobcat Station Wagon

The Bobcat Villager Wagon was unchanged for 1978. Priced at 4,244. FOB Detroit
(Below) The 1978 Standard Bobcat wagon with optional stylized wheels. <u>Note:</u>
the absence of bumper guards and bumper rub strip. It sold for $4,112.

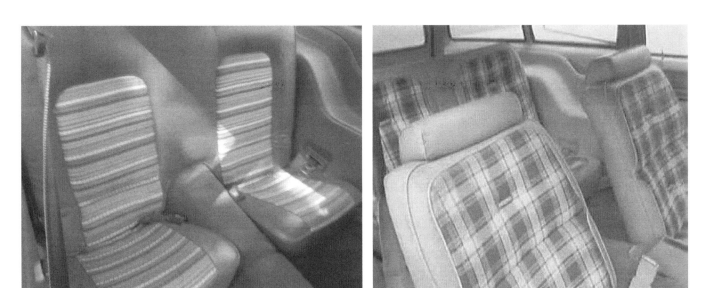

The 1978 Bobcat Wagon Interiors were available in all-vinyl or vinyl and cloth in bright stripe and plaid patterns. Bobcat front seat head rests were adjustable.

1979 Bobcat Station Wagon

Two trim lives were available in 1978. The Villager which had wood trimmed panels and framing similar to the Pinto and the Standard, shown below.

The 1977 Bobcat had a new grille and hood. Parking lamps were incorporated into the head light bezels. New interiors were also available. Plaid cloth was popular.

1980 Bobcat Station Wagon

1980 would be the final year for the Bobcat wagon. It was unchanged from the previous year. Two trim levels were once again available; the Villager and the Standard. The Standard sold for $5,070. and the Villager for $5,183.

The Villager shown here has optional wire wheel covers which were very popular. Instruments were positioned in front of the driver, one cluster housed the speedometer, the other the analog fuel gauge and idiot warning lights.

1975 Bobcat Station Wagon

Wheelbase: 94.8 Inches Engine: 140.0 cu in In-Line 4 cylinder, 83hp

Model	Price	Built
22 Villager Station Wagon 2-door	$3,481.	13,583

1976 Bobcat Station Wagon

Wheelbase: 94.8 Inches Engine: 140.0 cu in In-Line 4 cylinder, 83hp
Optional Engine: 170.8 cu in V-6, 100hp, Cruise-O-Matic Transmission

Model	Price	Built
22 Villager Station Wagon 2-door	$3,643.	18,731

1977 Bobcat Station Wagon

Wheelbase: 94.8 Inches Engine: 140.0 cu in In-Line 4 cyliner, 89hp
Optional Engine: 170.8 cu in V-6, 93hp, Cruise-O-Matiic Transmission

Model	Price	Built
22 Standard Wagon 2-door	$3,629.	}13,047
22 Villager Wagon 2-door	$3,771.	

1978 Bobcat Station Wagon

Wheelbase: 94.8 Inches Engine: 140.0 cu in In-Line 4cylinder, 88hp
Optional Engine: 170.8 cu in V-6, 90hp, Cruise-O-Matic Transmission

Model	Price	Built
22 Standard Wagon 2-door	$4,112.	}8,840
22 Villager Wagon 2-door	$4,244.	

1979 Bobcat Station Wagon

Wheelbase: 94.8 Inches Engine: 140.0 cu in In-Line 4 cylinder, 88hp
Optional Engine: 170.8 cu in V-6, 102hp, Cruise-O-Matic Transmission

Model	Price	Built
22 Standard Wagon 2-door	$4,410.	}9,119
22 Villager Wagon 2-door	$4,523.	

1980 Bobcat Station Wagon

Wheelbase: 94.8 Inches Engine: 140.0 cu in In-Line 4 cylinder, 88hp

Model	Price	Built
22 Standard Wagon 2-door	$5,070.	}5,547
22 Villager Wagon 2-door	$5,183.	

Pricing and production information from Encyclopedia of American Cars Consumers Guide.

Pontiac Astre Hatchback GT

Some of the features shown are optional at extra cost.

Economy never looked better

Who says an economy car has to be an import? Who says economy can't be beautiful?

The 1974 Astre from Pontiac is our Canadian-built small economy car...and economy never looked better. Astre has stepped out and ahead of the usual "economy car" connotations. It looks great! Maybe Astre looks more expensive than it is. But, what's wrong with that?

Pontiac Astre Safari Station Wagon

Standard plaid cloth interior

Astre is priced below many of the top selling import models. And Astre is economical in so many ways. The lightweight aluminum engine is easy on gas, and gives you all the get-up-and-go you need.

Buckle up for safety

Astre is comfortable, with Premier plaid cloth-and-vinyl trim on deep full-foam seats. And the head and leg room rivals many bigger cars. Find out for yourself.

Astre comes in three models: a Coupe, a Hatchback, and a Safari Station Wagon.

The 1974 Astre from Pontiac... economy never looked better.

PONTIAC Astre
Right on for 1974

121

Astre/Sunbird (Pontiac)
1975-1979

In 1975 at the height of the oil embargoes, in desperate need of of an economy car, to satisfy the mpg requirement mandated by the government; Pontiac finally entered the U.S. Sub-Compact market with the Astre,; which had been selling in Canada since 1973. The Astre was a variant of the Chevrolet Vega with a different face and interior. Initially there was a hatchback, notchback, three levels of a wagon and a panel delivery which only sold in Canada.

The wagons were designated: the "S" Safari wagon, the Safari Wagon and the "SJ" Safari Wagon. The three wagons differed in trim and performance. For 1975-76 the Astre was powered by the Vega 140.0 cu.in. 4 cylinder engine. In 1977 a 151 cu.in. was available. Depending on the trim level you could order a 3-speed manual transmission, a 4-speed manual, a 5-speed manual and a Turbo-Hydramatic 3-speed automatic.

The entry level Safari wagon was the "S" model and the "SJ" was the top of the line Safari which featured soft nylon upholstery, cut pile carpeting, padded door panels, a fabric headliner, rally instruments and the 4-speed manual or Turbo Hydramatic. Additionally a GT package was available which combined the "S" interior with the "SJ" performance.

A combined total of 15,322 Astre Safari wagons were sold in 1975. The Panel Delivery was discontinued at the end of 1975 and only a single series Astre Safari was available for 1976. The 1976 model received extensive anti-rust and integrity improvements along with a new grille. Sales fell to 13,125.

1977, its final year, the Astre received a minor facelift. A new vertical grille and optional 13 inch aluminum wheels, along with a new engine. In 1978 the Astre was replaced by the Sunbird. The Sunbird Safari wagon continued through 1979. For its entire run, 1975-1979 50,114 wagons were sold. In the end the Astre was plagued with the same problems as the Vega, which did not help its sales.

1975 Astre Station Wagon

The 1975 Safari wagon, one, of three wagon models available. An all-vinyl interior with high back bucket seats was standard. Wood grain exterior side panels, stylized wheels and roof rack were optional. The mid level Safari was priced at $3,175. A grand total of all wagon models sold the first year was only 15,322.

The Safari "S" the bare bones entry level Astre wagon for 1975. Priced at $3,071.

1976 Astre Station Wagon

Due to poor sales in 1975 only one model was available in 1976 the Safari. The decal wood paneling was optional, along with the roof rack and stylized wheels. Note: the accent strips on the tail gate a retro carry over from the 1950s.

1977 Astre Station Wagon

1977 marked the final year for the Astre there were no changes. Only one model was available. The decal wood grain paneling was optional. Only 10,341 were sold

1978 Sunbird Station Wagon

Introduced in 1978 the Sunbird Safari wagon looked like the Astre. Everything about it was Astre, including the interior-buyers were not fooled, only 8,424 were sold at a price tag of $3,741.

1979 Sunbird Station Wagon

The 1979 Sunbird Sport wagon was priced at $4,321 and 2,002 were sold. This was the last year for the Pontiac Sub-Compact, it was a versatile wagon which could accommodate a whole soccer team. The perfect suburban second car.

1975 Astre Station Wagon

Wheelbase: 97.0 Inches Engine: 140.0 cu in In-Line 4 cylinder, 78hp

Optional Engine: 140.0 cu in In-Line 4 cylinder, 87hp

Model	Price	Built
C15 "S" Safari Wagon 2-door	$3,071.	
V15 Safari Wagon 2-door	$3,175.	}15,322
X15 "SJ" Safari Wagon 2-door	$3,686.	

1976 Astre Station Wagon

Wheelbase: 97.0 Inches Engine: 140.0 cu in In-Line 4 cylinder, 70hp

Optional Engine: 140.0 cu in In-Line 4 cylinder, 84hp

Model	Price	Built
C15 Safari Wagon 2-door	$3,306.	13,125

1977 Astre Station Wagon

Wheelbase: 97.0 Inches Engine: 140.0 cu in In-Line 4 cylinder, 84hp

Optional Engine: 151.0 cu in In-Line 4 cylinder, 87hp

Model	Price	Built
C15 Safari Wagon 2-door	$3,595	10,341

1978 Sunbird Station Wagon

Wheelbase 97.0 Inches Engine: 151.0 cu in In-Line 4 cylinder, 85hp

Optional Engine: 231.0 cu in V-8 cylinder, 105hp

Model	Price	Built
M15 Safari Wagon 2-door	$3,741	8,424

1979 Sunbird Station Wagon

Wheelbase: 97.0 Inches Engine: 151.0 cu in In-Line 4cylinder, 85hp

Model	Price	Built
M15 Safari Sport Wagon 2-door	$4,321.	2,902

Pricing and production infromation from the Encyclopedia of American Cars, by Editors of Consumers Guide.

Pacer (AMC)
1977-1980

AMC introduced the Pacer in 1975, as a up-scale companion to the short wheel base Gremlin. The initial model was a hatchback coupe with a 100 inch wheelbase. Four inches longer than the Germlin. The design concept was similar to the British Mini Cooper, large on the inside and small on the outside. The width was 77.3 inches comparable to a large full size sedan The pacer had a low belt line, and large oversized windows. The glass area provided unparalleled visibility. The Pacer lines were smooth and rounded, giving the car a futuristic look. One of its standard features was a roof rack.

In its inaugural year the Pacer Hatchback Coupe, powered by a 232.0 cu in. 100hp, in-line 6cylinder engine*, priced at $3,299. it sold 72,158 units. Additional features included a electronic ignition, front disc brakes and a 22 gallon gas tank.

In 1977 a Pacer station wagon was added. The over-all body length was increased while the wheelbase remained the same 100 inches. The standard engine continued to be the 232 cu in, 6 cylinder engine. Horsepower had been reduced to 88hp. Priced at $3,709, a total of 37,999 were sold. The Pacer wagon was a 3-door model. two front doors and a rear hatch. A unique feature; the passenger door was nearly 4 inches wider than the driver door. A roof rack was standard.

For 1978 Pacer offered a standard 6 cylinder model and a DL V-8 model. The standard sold for $4,193. and the DL for $4,443. It was face lifted with a new grille.

In 1979 four new trim levels were available, the DL and the Limited in both the 6 cylinder and V-8 versions. Prices increased dramatically and sales dropped. 1980 marked the end of the Pacer. Only two trim levels were available, both in the 6 cylinder version.

---

*Originally the Pacer was designed to accept a Wankel Rotary engine, supplied by GM But when GM abandon the Wankle project, AMC installed their In-Line six and later a V-8.

Note: The Rambler American which succeeded the original Rambler, debuted a wagon in 1959 on the 100 inch wheelbase. And was available through 1963. AMC had no Sub-Compact wagon in the early 1970's. The American was essentially a continuation of the original Rambler.

1977 Pacer Wagon

The 1977 Pacer wagon arrived late to the Sub-Compact wagon wars of the 1970s. The single available model had a number of standard features not found in competitor models. It had a low belt line, large windows and the interior was as wide as a Cadillac sedan. It was often called "Fishbowl on wheels", "Pregnant Guppy" or Galssmobile". Its shape was inspired by a football.

The pacer featured pleated cloth and vinyl interior. Head rests were adjustable Rear seats folded for additional cargo space. The 1977 Pacer sold for $3,799.

1978 Pacer Station Wagon

For 1978 Pacer offered a standard 6 and the DL V-8. The 90hp 6 cylinder sold for $4,193 compared to the 88hp 4 cylinder Pinto Squire at $4,343.

1979 Pacer Station Wagon

The 1979 Pacer was available in two trim levels and two engine sizes. You had a choice of cloth or all-vinyl seat upholstery. Interiors were plush. Wood grin side panels gave way to two tone paint schemes. Sales continued to drop.

1980 Pacer Station Wagon

1980 would be the last year for the Pacer two trim levels were available, the DL and the Limited. The DL sold for $5,558, the Limited for $6,182 , only 1,341 sold.

1977 Pacer Wagon

Wheelbase: 100. Inches Engine: 232.0 cu in, In-Line 6 cylinder, 88hp

Model	Price	Built
68-7 Station Wagon	$3,202.	37,999

1978 Pacer Wagon

Wheelbase: 100 inches Engine: 232.0 cu in In-Line 6 cylinder, 90hp
Optional Engine: 304.0 cu in V-8, 130hp

Model	Price	Built
68-7 Station Wagon (6cyl)	$4,193.	}13,820
68-7 Station Wagon (V-8)	$4,443.	

1979 Pacer Wagon

Wheelbase: 100 Inches Engine: 258 cu in In-Line 6 cylinder, 100hp
Optional Engine: 304 cu in V-8, 125hp

Model	Price	Built
68-7 DL Wagon (6cyl)	$5,189	}7,352
68-7 Limited Wagon (6cyl)	$6,189	
68-7 DL Wagon (V-8)	$5,589	
68-7 Limited Wagon (V-8)	$6,589	

1980 Pacer Wagon

Wheelbase: 100 Inches Engine: 258 cu in In-Line 6 cylinder, 110hp

Model	Price	Built
68-5 DL Wagon (6cyl)	$5,558.	}1,341
68-7 Limited Wagon (6cyl)	$6,182.	

Pricing and production from Encyclopedia of American Cars by Consumers Guide And amcpacer.com

The 1978 AMC Pacer Wagon.
Now you can get the room and ride of a Pacer with the load space of a wagon.

Because it's a Pacer, you get the unique, wide design that provides so much more passenger room and comfort.

And Pacer's extra-wide stance, combined with rack and pinion steering and isolated suspension gives you a road-hugging stability, precise handling and an uncommonly smooth ride.

Because it's a wagon, you get plenty of utility and convenience. That unique wide design gives you wagon space without wagon waste. The rear hatch opens on a load floor that's wide and flat, so you can use it all. And you can create even more space by folding the rear seat down.

The '78 Pacer Wagon has many

The new AMC Pacer Wagon's unique wide design gives you wagon space without wagon waste.

luxurious features, too. Like individually reclining front seats, extra quiet insulation, wood grain instrument panel, electric clock and much more. All standard at no extra cost. So is the coverage of AMC's exclusive BUYER PROTECTION PLAN,® with the only full 12 month/12,000 mile warranty. That means AMC will fix or replace any part, except tires, whether the part is defective or just plain wears out under normal use and service.

So, if you want the convenience of a wagon, with the ride and comfort of a Pacer —you've got it.

The 1978 AMC Pacer Wagon.

AMC ◢ Pacer
The room and ride Americans want.
The size America needs.

Resources and References

Encyclopedia of American Cars
by Editors of Consumer Guide

Wikipedia.com

Howstuffworks.com

amcpacer.com

Crosleyautoclub.com

Standard Catalog of Chevrolet
by Pat Chappell

Encyclopedia of American Cars
by James H. Moloney

Standard Catalog of Ford
by John Gunnell

Standard Catalog of American
Cars, by Editors of Old Cars

Woodie Times-December 2004

SIA#200-April 2004

Vintage Truck-December 2013

Hemmings-August 2012

Great American Woodies and
Wagons by Donald Narus

Standard Catalog of Pontiac
by John Gunnell

About the Author

Don Narus is an Auto Historian and author of over twenty auto books, spanning more than four decades. His latest works can found at www.amazon.com, www.newalbanybooks.com, www.lulu.com, and barnesandnoble.com He splits his time between New Albany Ohio and Palm Harbor Florida. You can contact the author at djnarus@gmail.com

Other titles by Don Narus

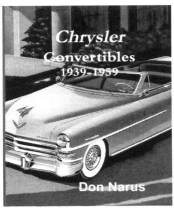

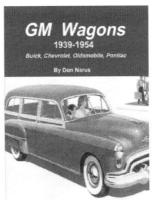
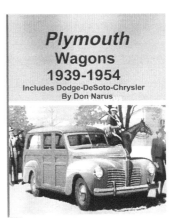

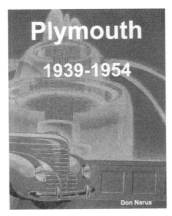
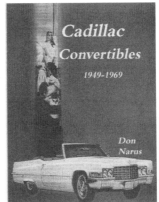
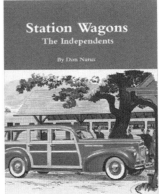

April 2014   **Sept 2014**